BUILDINGS

HOW THEY WORK

ROBERT ADAM

STERLING PUBLISHING CO. INC. NEW YORK

Managing Editor: Thomas Keegan
Editor: Nicky Barber
Design: David West Children's Book Design
Illustrators: Peter Kesteven; Mark Franklin;
Michael Steward; Michael Fisher (Garden
Studio); James Field, John York, Mike Taylor
(Simon Girling Associates); David Burroughs

Library of Congress Cataloging-in-Publication
Data Available

10 9 8 7 6 5 4 3 2 1

Published 1995 by Sterling Publishing
Company, Inc.
387 Park Avenue South, New York, N.Y. 10016
Originally published by Simon & Schuster
Young Books under the title *Buildings by
Design*
© 1994 by Simon & Schuster Young Books
Distributed in Canada by Sterling Publishing
% Canadian Manda Group, One Atlantic
Avenue, Suite 105
Toronto, Ontario, Canada M6K 3E7
*Typeset by Goodfellow and Egan Ltd
Printed and bound in Portugal*

Sterling ISBN 0-8069-0958-7

CON

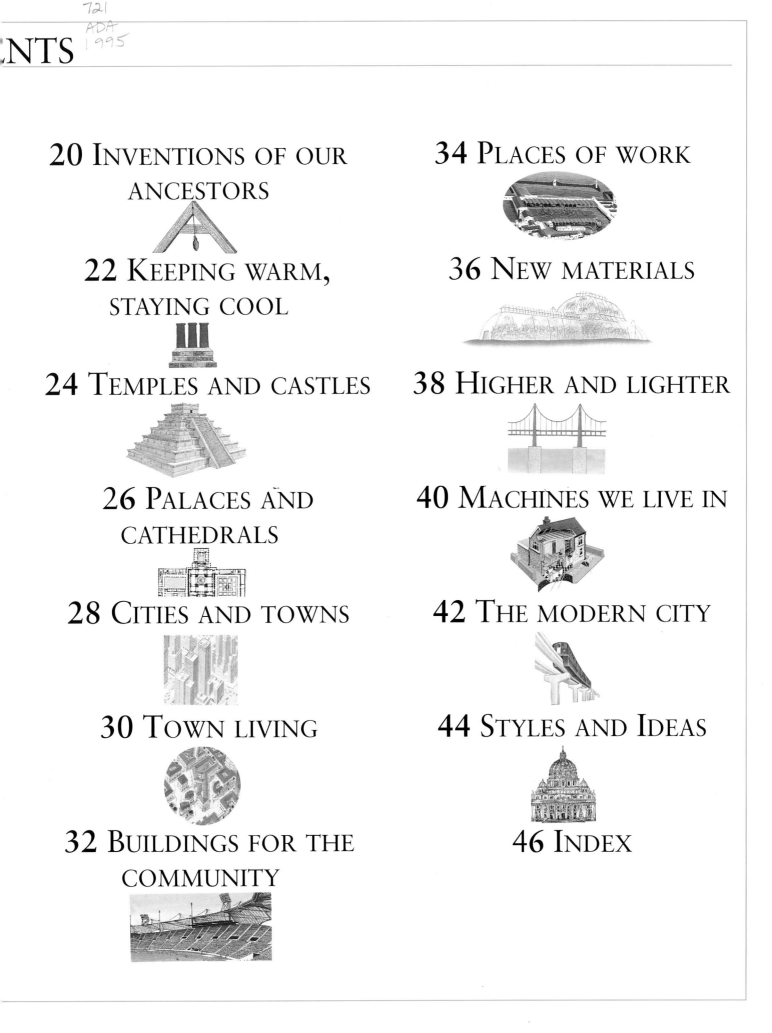

PEOPLE AND BUILDINGS

We all live in buildings. People lived in buildings long before they invented writing or learned to use the wheel. Buildings provide essential shelter from the weather. They are also built to fit in with the way of life of the people who use them. The way that people in a community design and construct their buildings is an important part of how that community organizes its life together. The design of buildings tells people how they are to be used and how important they are. As different types of design have taken shape over the centuries, each community has been given an individual character. As we all grow up and learn to know our own buildings, their design can make us feel at home with our surroundings.

The Forbidden City
For centuries, the Chinese people believed that their emperors were gods. The Chinese emperors lived in a special private city called the Forbidden City. It was built in the middle of the capital city, Beijing, nearly 600 years ago. It had high walls and a moat to keep out the ordinary people who were not allowed even to look at the emperor. The Forbidden City had large buildings for special ceremonies, set out in a formal plan. The shape, color and position of each building had a religious message. The rule of the last emperor ended over 80 years ago. Today, the Forbidden City is open for the public to walk around.

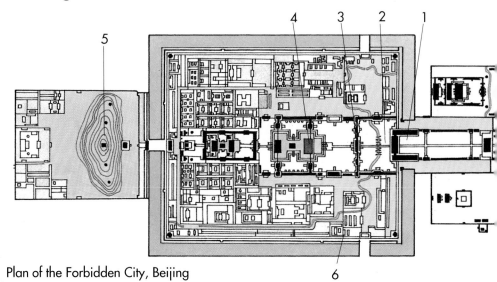

Plan of the Forbidden City, Beijing

T'ai-ho Tien (Hall of Supreme Harmony), Forbidden City

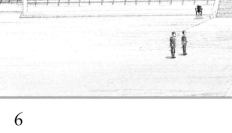

Life in a West African village

In parts of West Africa, people live with their relations in groups of huts. The huts are made of mud. Each building is designed for a particular purpose. One building will store grain, one will be for cooking, another will be where women sleep, another will be for unmarried men. Sometimes a building will have a special shape for its purpose. The group of buildings may look disorganized but each hut has a particular position as well as special features and decorations which are part of the traditional ceremonies of the people.

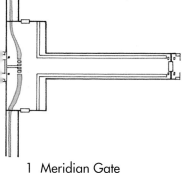

1 Meridian Gate
2 Golden Water Bridge
3 Gatehouse
4 T'ai-ho Tien
5 Coal Hill
6 Moat

Piazza della Signoria, Florence

News from the piazza

Italian life has always been lively and public. Five hundred years ago Italian cities were rich and famous. People met in their public squares, or piazzas, to discuss the news and gossip of the day. Important citizens showed their wealth and taste by putting up statues and fountains, and by building fine houses and churches in the piazzas. These beautiful places have inspired generations of artists and architects. People in Italy still meet in the piazzas to talk and gossip.

WAYS OF LIVING

We work and play in buildings that are made to fit the way we live. If our lives are simple, the houses we make for ourselves will also be simple. If we want to impress people we will decorate our houses and make them as big as possible.

The size and shape of a building is determined by the way people want to use it. As people's needs and wishes change so their buildings change also. When we look at buildings of the past we can see in them the lives, customs, fortunes and ideas of the people for whom they were built.

Cooking fire

Cottage

Chatsworth House, Derbyshire, England, 1696

Life in a cottage

Two centuries ago in Britain, most ordinary people lived in primitive conditions in small houses or cottages. These cottages were usually made from local materials. They had floors of earth and cooking was done on an open fire. There was no glass in the windows and little furniture. All the family slept in one room, and often their animals lived in another part of the house.

The Theatre, Chatsworth

Wealthy life styles

Wealthy families have always built big houses for themselves, designed in the latest fashion and using the best materials. Inside, these houses had large rooms for entertaining guests with dinner and dancing. The bedrooms were furnished with four-poster beds covered with expensive cloth. All the rooms were richly decorated, and the walls were hung with fine paintings. Many servants were needed to clean, cook and wait on the family and guests. The servants had rooms in the cellars and top floors. But the servants lived better than the ordinary farm workers in their cottages.

The Painted Room, Chatsworth

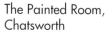

A bedroom, Chatsworth

Modern house

Modern ways of living

Today, many people live in small, modern houses. Huge housing developments have been built in the last 50 years. A modern house is divided into small rooms, each with its own special use. There are one or two bathrooms, and kitchens are fitted with cupboards. Machines for washing and cleaning make life convenient, and new houses are well heated and insulated against the cold. Each house usually has a small garden and a place to park a car.

Unchanging designs

Sometimes the way we use a building gives it a shape that hardly changes over the centuries. The Romans built amphitheaters to watch their cruel sports. Modern sports stadiums are the same shape as Roman amphitheaters because this is the best design for allowing crowds of people to get a good view.

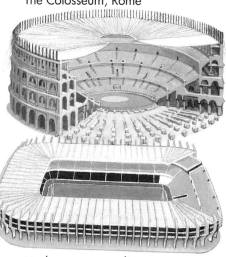

The Colosseum, Rome

Modern sports stadium

Changing designs

Farm buildings are completely practical. The way they look is decided by their use. Old barns had big doors in the middle. During threshing, the draft from the open doors would blow the light husks away from the heavy grains of corn. Today, the corn is harvested, separated and dried with machines. It is kept in tall stores called silos.

Barn   Silo

Shelter

Like many animals, people need shelter to survive. In the same way that birds make nests for their young, and animals make burrows for protection, people need to make houses. Houses provide people with shelter from the effects of heat, cold and rain as they sleep, rest, eat and bring up children. The earliest types of shelter were easy to put up and take down as people moved from place to place in search of food. In places where food could be found or farmed all the year round it was worth making the effort to put up more permanent shelter. Although modern buildings seem to be more complicated than these early shelters, their first purpose is still to keep out the weather and to protect whatever is going on inside.

Cave dwellings

Before people built solid shelters they would sometimes use a cave as a home. Bears and other animals also lived in caves. Often, caves were used by people only in the winter. A fire in the entrance to the cave kept out animals and was used for cooking and warmth. Some caves were lived in for thousands of years and people decorated the walls with paintings.

Reed house

Weaverbird's nest

Cave dwelling

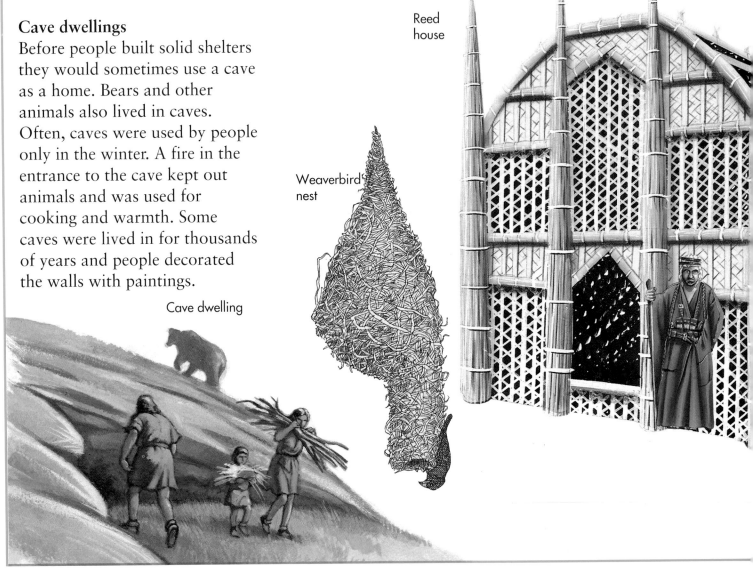

A reed house

Thousands of years ago people built lightweight shelters, which have since disappeared. In some parts of the world, however, people still build shelters of grasses and other simple materials. In the wet marshes of Iraq large houses are built of reeds. The reeds are tied together in bundles and bent over to join in the middle. The walls are made of woven reeds and the roofs of reed mats. These houses are skilfully built and decorated. They are so light they can float on large rafts like islands. The weaverbird also builds a simple shelter out of grass. Using its feet and beak it weaves a nest around supporting branches.

The native American tepee

The native Americans who lived on the plains hunted buffalo and had to follow the herds as they moved around. Their shelters needed to be light, and easy to put up and take down. The native Americans used a tent, called a tepee, which was supported on 15 poles and covered with as many as 20 buffalo hides, all sewn together.

Termite nests

Tepee

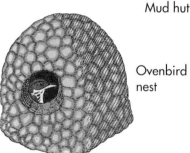

Grass roof

Mud hut

Mud houses

In many parts of the world people build shelters out of earth or dried mud, with roofs of grass or thatch. The roof keeps the walls dry. Termites too, make nests from mud with sloping roofs to keep off the rain. The ovenbird also makes a nest out of mud.

Ovenbird nest

Flats

Sometimes people share their shelter. Building several houses under one roof saves a lot of space. People have lived close together like this for practical reasons, or to defend themselves, for centuries. In modern towns people often live together in blocks of flats. In North America, prairie dogs also live together for defence, digging underground burrows with separate rooms.

Prairie dog burrow

CLIMATE

People have adapted the design of their shelters for different climates. This has allowed people to live all over the world. From the snows of the Arctic to the hottest deserts, wherever there is food, people have learned to build shelters designed specially to keep out the worst of the weather. There are lots of ingenious ways of building protection from the weather and making the best use of the climate. Over the centuries, these simple and useful inventions have given traditional buildings their own special character.

Warm inside a yurt

The wide, open expanses of land in the center of Asia can be very cold. People travel from place to place taking their animals to fresh grass. They take with them their portable houses, called yurts. Yurts have walls of thick cloth or felt, made by beating loose wool into a heavy mat. The walls are held up by a criss-cross fence, and bent poles support the roof. When a fire is lit inside, the felt covering keeps in the heat and makes the yurt warm and cozy.

Yurt

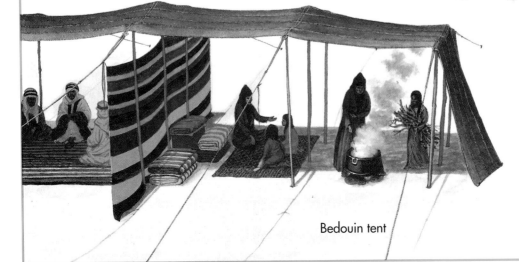

Bedouin tent

Bedouin tents

The Bedouin people live in the hot deserts of the Middle East and North Africa. They live in tents made of woven cloth.

One wall of the tent is put up to provide protection against the wind. Other walls are left open to allow a gentle breeze to cool the inside of the tent.

Stilt houses

In parts of Southeast Asia the land is covered in a dense growth of trees. The climate is hot and steamy. People live by the sides of lakes and rivers where they fish for food. They build their houses on stilts so that when the water level rises the houses are not flooded. People move from house to house in boats.

Overhanging roofs

In the mountains of Switzerland there is heavy snow in the winter. Swiss chalets are built with steep roofs that overhang the walls of the building on all sides. The overhang protects balconies underneath from falling snow. Hay to feed the cattle in the winter used to be hung outside and kept dry by the roof.

Overhanging roof

Swiss chalet

Keeping the roof on

On the west coast of Ireland strong winds blow straight off the Atlantic Ocean. The weather is often very wet. Cottages were built of heavy stones with thatched roofs. The thatch on the roofs was held down against the wind by ropes attached to boulders.

Stones to hold thatch down

Living underground

In one area of North Africa where the weather is hot and dry some people live in underground houses. These houses are cut out of soft rock. The rooms in the houses face into a central underground courtyard which is always in the shade. This design makes the houses pleasantly cool inside. Some animals also use the shade to stay cool. This lizard shelters from the sun underneath a stone.

NATURAL MATERIALS

In early times, shelters were made from materials that could be found nearby. People looked at the land around them for whatever was convenient and practical to put up their buildings. They used many materials, from stones to logs, from skins to leaves. How effective their buildings were at keeping out or controlling the climate depended on what materials were easily available. The problems and expense of moving heavy loads over land often limited the choice of materials to what was near at hand. In coastal areas, however, buildings were often made from better materials than those found locally, which could be brought from distant places by boat. In more recent times, improvements in transport and cheap fuel have made it possible to build with materials brought from almost anywhere in the world.

Caddis fly larvae

Steel beam

Stone protection

In some areas near the sea or by rivers, stones are broken up by the movement of the water into just the right size for building. These boulders and slates can be used to make solid buildings. The caddis fly larva also finds small pebbles or other materials from the river bed and covers itself with them for protection.

Snow houses

In the Arctic the native people of the region, the Inuit, build their houses, called igloos, out of solid blocks of ice. Igloos are skilfully constructed in a dome which holds the ice together and is the best shape for keeping in the heat. The ice is so thick that igloos do not melt even when small fires are lit inside them.

Tailorbird nest

A waterproof hut

It is hot and damp in tropical jungles. People weave together branches from trees and the huge leaves of tropical plants to make waterproof huts. The Asian tailorbird also uses leaves for shelter, stitching them together to make a nest.

Beaver's lodge

Making steel

Iron ore is dug out of the ground in certain places in the world. The iron ore is turned into steel by heating in a furnace. The steel is then rolled into shape before it cools. Today, ships, trains and trucks carry steel beams and posts for building all over the world.

Log shelters

In Canada and other northern countries there are huge areas of pine forest. Log cabins are made from the whole trunks of pine trees which have been cut down to make a clearing. The trunks are flattened on two sides and cut at the ends to fit together. The roof is covered with cedar wood cut into thin tiles, called shingles. The Canadian beaver also uses logs to build shelters, called lodges.

MAKING WALLS

The first part of a building to be put up is the wall. Walls can be made of many different materials. There is a different way of putting each material together to give it enough strength to hold up the roof and keep out the weather. Walls must be built on solid ground. If the ground is weak, foundations have to be put below the walls to make the building safe. All modern buildings have foundations. Walls in houses also have doors and windows. For each type of material and method of building there is a special way of holding up the wall over the opening above a door or window.

Daub   Wattle   Timber supports

Wedge-shaped bricks

Flemish bond

Wattle and daub
Old houses in England often had walls made from a woven fence of thin branches (called wattle) fitted between timber supports. A mixture of straw, mud and manure (called daub) was added on each side.

Brickwork
Bricks have been used all over the world for thousands of years. Bricks are quite thin and are usually laid two thick to give the wall extra strength. The way the bricks are fitted together is called the bond. Wedge-shaped bricks which stay up by pressing against one another are used above an opening in a brick wall. Modern brick walls usually have two layers with a gap, or cavity, in-between. The inside layer is made of insulating blocks which keep in the heat.

Uneven stones
Early Greek builders and the Incas in South America did not cut stones to a regular size before building a wall. Instead, each stone was cut to a special shape to fit the stones next to it.

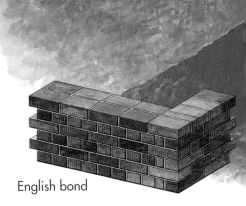

English bond

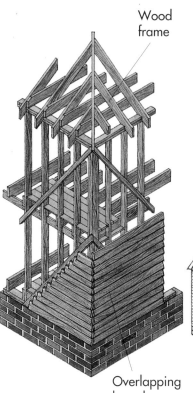

Wood frame

Overlapping boards

Frame Houses

In North America, many houses have wooden walls. These are made from thin, upright studs set close together between plates at the top and bottom. The studs are often tied together and braced with longer pieces on a diagonal.

Rammed earth walls

Mud walls are found all over the world. Mud or earth is put between wooden boards and rammed down to make it firm. This is done in layers until the wall is complete. Mud walls have to be thick and protected on the outside with plaster to stay up. Openings for doors and windows are made with wooden beams.

Making an arch

Most stone walls are made from squared stones cut to a regular size and laid in even layers or courses. These stone walls can have quite wide openings with arches over the top. The stones in an arch are each cut to a wedge shape and laid on to a wood frame. When the last stone is in place the frame can be taken away. The arch will push the weight from the wall above to the sides of the opening.

Foundations

Insulating blocks

Wood frame

These stones knocked away once arch is complete

Stretcher bond

Cavity wall

17

KEEPING UP THE ROOF

Adding a roof makes four walls into a building and a shelter. A roof keeps out the sun and rain, and creates a space for people to live in. The covering on the roof can be light, such as thatch, or heavy, such as clay tiles. In dry climates roofs can be flat, in wet climates they are steep to throw off the rain. Different methods of making roofs have been found for the different types of material used for building. People used great skill and invention when they fitted together natural materials to make the first specially designed beams and the first domes.

Corbeled domes

Early domes, like early arches, were made by stepping or corbeling each layer of stone inwards. Circular buildings were constructed with the walls gradually stepped inwards until they met at the top. Domes made this way were not usually round but pointed, so that each step could be small and even. But unless the stones were very long, only quite small buildings could be covered with this type of dome.

A flat roof

Wood is light, and does not break easily when it bends. It can be used to cover large spaces. In places where there is little rainfall, a flat wooden roof is simple to build. In a hot country a flat roof can also be used as a roof terrace. Early flat roofs had beams set side-by-side covered with a layer of mud (*see below*). Later roofs used less wood by spacing the beams further apart and laying tiles or boards between them.

Corbeled dome

Wooden beams

Mud

Building a round dome

Round domed roofs could be built if the dome was made of shaped stones or bricks, like an arch. The weight of the roof pressing down on the dome would hold the wedge-shaped stones or bricks together by forcing them to press against one another. In the Middle East there was very little timber available to support the dome while it was being built. To solve this problem, people in the Middle East put up their domes so that they stood up even when only partly built.

Pitched roofs

Sloping or pitched roofs can be covered with tiles and will keep out heavy rain. A pitched roof is made out of wooden beams that are joined together to make a frame.

A Chinese pitched roof

Chinese pitched roofs are supported on beams and posts joined together to make a square framework. At the top corners of each square a beam runs along the length of the roof. These beams hold up smaller beams or rafters which follow the curved slope of the roof and support the tiles.

A European truss roof

In Europe a type of pitched roof was developed which used less wood than the Chinese roof to cover wider spaces. Wooden beams were joined to make a frame or truss which had horizontal, vertical and diagonal beams. The diagonal beams made the truss stronger by taking the weight from the roof more effectively to the side walls. Today, most wooden pitched roofs use this kind of truss.

Vertical beam (post)

Horizontal beam

Truss roof

Diagonal beam

Chinese pitched roof

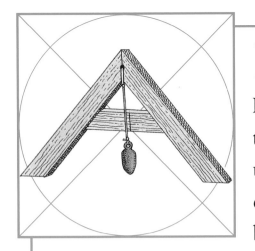

INVENTIONS OF OUR ANCESTORS

Putting up any building involves changing and fitting together natural materials. At first, people put up houses using the materials they found around them. But as communities became more organized, some people began to specialize in putting up buildings. Building workers took natural materials and changed them in different ways to make them easier to use. Some materials were burned or mixed together to turn them into something more solid. Others were fitted together in new ways to make them stronger or lighter. Thousands of years ago, people made inventions that eventually took building from the construction of simple shelters to the creation of great monuments.

Firing clay

Instead of making walls of solid clay, people found that clay could be dried in the sun to make bricks. In about 2000BC it was discovered that bricks heated to a high temperature in an oven or kiln were even stronger. The same burnt clay could be shaped into thin tiles for roofs.

Roof tiles

Brick kiln

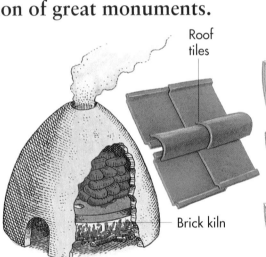

Machines for building

To make larger buildings, stones and other heavy loads had to be raised to the top of the building work. At first, people used ramps to pull up stones. But the ancient Romans invented a crane that used ropes threaded through wooden beams and wound round a big wheel to raise the stones up to the top of the building. This crane was one of the first machines designed to make building work easier.

The first cement

Two thousand years ago, the ancient Romans discovered that when they mixed ash from volcanos with water and a type of burned chalk called lime, the mixture became hard when it dried. This was the first cement. Using this invention, the Romans could build huge, solid buildings. One of these buildings, the Pantheon, is still standing in Rome. The Pantheon is 141 feet high and 141 feet wide.

All the light comes through a hole in the roof.

Stone vaulting

The Pantheon, Rome

Hole in roof

Stone vaulting

In the Middle Ages, the people who designed cathedrals wanted to build high stone roofs and put big stained glass windows in the walls. To do this, they needed to make the roof as light as possible. They invented a roof with two pointed arches which crossed over each other and rested their weight on thin columns. Once the arches had been built, a thin skin of stone was laid between them. This way of building a stone roof is called vaulting.

Stone "skin"

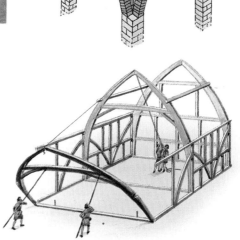

Putting up a wooden frame

The main frame of a wooden building is often made on the ground. The parts of the frame can then be pulled up and joined together to make a complete frame. The walls and roof are fixed on to this frame.

A wooden joint

KEEPING WARM, STAYING COOL

Sometimes, keeping out the weather is not enough and a building needs to be made warmer or cooler inside. For thousands of years, people have burned wood, coal, peat and even animal dung in their houses to keep warm. In hot countries, people have used cooling breezes and fountains to stay cool. Today, we can heat and cool our buildings by using electricity that is made by burning fuel in distant power stations. However, the smoke from these fires is harming the planet and people are now looking for ways to keep warm and cool without burning fuel.

Roman central heating
Some ancient Roman houses had central heating. The floors were held up by brick pillars. On one side of the house a fire was kept burning by slaves. The smoke from the fire went through hollow bricks in the walls and the warm air was drawn across the space under the floor. The Romans also heated their rooms with open charcoal fires in metal stoves called braziers.

Smoke

Hollow bricks

Fire

Warm air

Brick pillars

A warm fire
To keep warm inside, people brought fires into their houses. At first the fire stood in the middle of the floor, and smoke from the fire found its way out through a hole in the roof. This made the inside of the house very smoky. Later, chimneys were used to take the smoke out.

Victorian stove

22

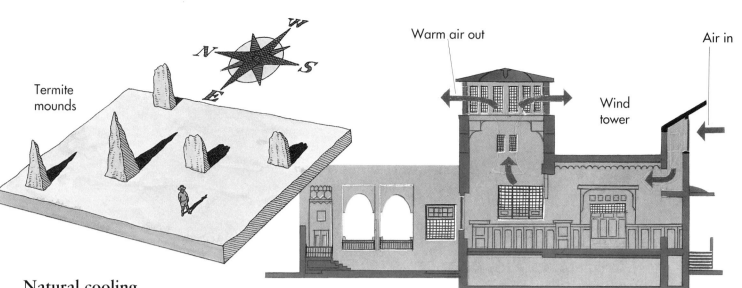

Termite mounds

Warm air out

Air in

Wind tower

Natural cooling

In the hot countries of the Middle East a type of natural cooling is used to make houses more comfortable. Above each house there is a tower to catch the wind. The wind is carried down into the house to create a breeze. In Australia, termites also build towers in a special way to control the temperature inside. These towers or mounds are thin and flat. They are carefully positioned so that the hot midday sun does not overheat them.

Electricity from a power station

Today, we can keep warm or cool without having to burn a fire or use the wind in our houses. Instead, the fire is burned far away at a power station. An engine or turbine changes the energy from the heat of the fire into electricity. Most power stations burn oil, coal or gas. But power stations can also use nuclear energy, wind power or energy from the tides. The electricity is taken through wires from the power station to thousands of buildings. Once the electricity is in a building it can be turned back into heat.

Using the sun's energy

Heat energy from the sun (solar energy) can be used to help with the heating of a building. The heat is collected in a solar panel. The panel has rows of thin pipes containing water. It is mounted on the roof and pointed towards the sun. As the water heats up it is pumped into the house. In countries with little sunshine, solar energy will not provide all the heat that is needed for a building. But it can be used together with another heating system, in order to save fuel.

Power station

Pipes

Solar panel

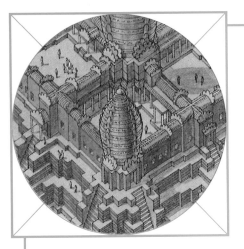

TEMPLES AND CASTLES

Like packs of animals, people probably always fought for hunting territory both with each other and with other animals. As people began to settle in one place they built fences and walls around their villages to defend their homes. Soon, people were also putting up fortresses for protection and defense. Once people were safely settled in a place they would build a house for their gods. These buildings are called temples. So, the first special buildings which were not used just as places to live were fortresses and temples.

Designing a fortress

The design of a fortress is a matter of life and death. The fortress must keep out invaders. Before the invention of gunpowder this meant building high, thick walls often with towers as strong points. Where possible, a fortress was built on a hill or surrounded with water. A large fortress also had to have space inside the main walls for soldiers to live and for stores. Some animals also build fortresses. This stick rat makes nests of sticks to keep intruders out.

Krak des Chevaliers, fortress in Syria

Stick rat

Stonehenge

Stonehenge was a temple built about 3000 years ago in Wiltshire, England. It was changed several times and used for at least 500 years. Nobody knows exactly what it was for, but it was probably used for the worship of the sun or the seasons. The stone circles probably marked out the sacred area.

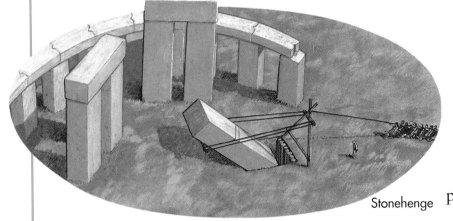

Stonehenge

24

Great Zimbabwe

In Zimbabwe in Africa there are ancient ruins of walled settlements. The biggest of these is called Great Zimbabwe. The settlements have been abandoned for centuries, but they are the only large stone ruins in southern Africa. The local stone was used to make large fortified areas with houses, stores and high walls. The people were obviously very skilled in building. The high, strong walls enclosing the other buildings were probably a defense against attack.

Ruins of Great Zimbabwe

An Aztec ziggurat

Inside the Parthenon

Temples

Temples are the houses of gods. Inside a temple there was a statue of the god for whom the temple was built, and gifts given to the god. Often only priests and kings were allowed to go into the temple. Worship and sacrifices took place at altars outside. To persuade the god to protect them, people would make sure that the temple was the best design and built of the best materials. Sometimes a temple was raised by building it on top of an artificial hill, called a ziggurat.

A Greek temple: the Parthenon, Athens

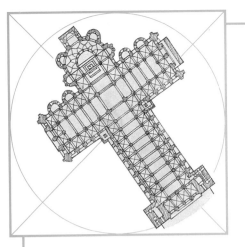

PALACES AND CATHEDRALS

As villages grew into towns, chiefs became kings and their houses became palaces. It was important for a palace to be large and impressive so that everyone could see that the kingdom was rich and powerful. The palace also had to have enough space for all the king's and queen's servants and administrators. As a result, palaces became large and complicated buildings. Temples also became larger as some religions brought people inside the house of their god to worship. Temples changed from large houses to huge public halls.

Meeting in the synagogue
The Jewish religion was one of the first to bring all its people together in a public hall. Buildings for the Jewish community to meet and worship are called synagogues. Meeting together to worship also became part of the Christian and Muslim religions.

The Escorial, Madrid

1 Palace
2 Church
3 University
4 Monastery
5 Library

An early synagogue

A carefully planned palace
Over 400 years ago, the Spanish king Philip II built a huge palace outside Madrid. It is called the Escorial. Inside the walls of the palace there is a church, a monastery, a university and a library. The king had his own private rooms behind the altar of the church, built to a plain design to show his religious faith.

Cathedrals and mosques

Christian churches and Muslim mosques needed to be large enough for everyone to pray together. Early mosques were large covered areas, often with rows of columns to hold up the roof. But the inside of a cathedral had to be open to let everyone see the ceremonies around the altar.

St Sophia, Istanbul

Dome roof

Open space

Columns

Inside the mosque at Cordoba, Spain

The palace at Knossos, Crete

1 Central court
2 Grand staircase
3 Throne room
4 Storerooms

A Cretan palace

The royal palace at Knossos in Crete was built about 3500 years ago. It is made up of a lot of small buildings, some four storeys high, around a central court. It seems unplanned, although it is very large. Some of the rooms are big enough for royal ceremonies, others were used as large food stores.

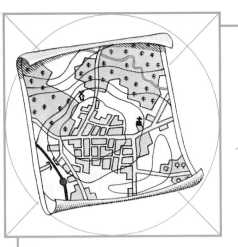

CITIES AND TOWNS

About 9000 years ago in the Middle East, people living in small communities began to exchange spare food for specialized skills. As these skills developed, people became shopkeepers, craftspeople, builders, school teachers and artists. This development happened partly because people lived together in towns and cities. It is how civilization began. Life in a town was often safer and more comfortable than in the country. There was more variety, with organized sports and entertainment. It is the way of life many people enjoy today.

From small beginnings

The ancient Romans built new towns in many parts of their empire. These towns were carefully planned. Streets and buildings were set out in a square plan, called a grid, inside the city walls. Roads and sewers were built, and a public area was made in the center with markets, courts and temples.

Growing up

As time went on more and more houses were built. Wealthy citizens, and sometimes emperors, also paid for grand public buildings to be put up.

A modern city

Most of New York was planned around a square "grid" pattern of roads. It quickly became a rich and important city and soon filled the island of Manhattan. As land in the city became expensive, houses were divided up into apartments, and skyscrapers were built to make best use of the land. Today, millions of people work and live in New York.

A medieval town

In the Middle Ages towns often grew up around a castle or a church, in places where a market was held. The first buildings would be built around the marketplace or alongside the roads that led to the market. These buildings were often the shops and houses of traders. But as these towns grew, there were often problems with sewage and the supply of water. Sometimes the towns became so dirty and smelly that people died from diseases. Then the mayor would try to improve conditions by making laws to control building work, and by putting in sewers.

A large town

Eventually all the space inside the city walls was used up. In places where there was no threat of attack, houses were built outside the walls. In the center, larger buildings were divided up.

TOWN LIVING

Town houses are different from country houses. Land for building in towns and cities is often very expensive, so town houses must be designed to make the best use of whatever space and daylight is available. Sometimes shops and places of work share the same building as houses. In more recent times, new inventions have made it possible for large numbers of people to live and work together by constructing higher and more complicated buildings.

Medieval town house

Roman town house

Viking house

Town houses through history
In ancient cities, houses were often built behind walls, hiding them from the street. The living rooms were arranged around open courts for light and air. Roman houses had two kinds of court. One was an atrium with an open roof to collect rainwater, and the other was a small, private garden.

After the Romans, towns often grew up from villages. People like the Vikings built their town houses in the same way as their country houses. As time went on, special types of narrow houses were built end-on to the street so that there could be more shops. Later medieval houses had street fronts that could overhang the street, also to gain more space.

By the end of the Middle Ages many Italian towns were large, important places. The noble families of the town lived in grand buildings with their relations and servants. Noble families were often fierce rivals, fighting each other for power. They built their houses to look impressive and safe, competing against each other to have the best design.

About 300 years ago, as Britain became rich through trade and industry, many British towns grew quite quickly. Houses were built in long rows. Today, many people live in towns and cities. The invention of new ways of building has made it possible to put up tall apartments.

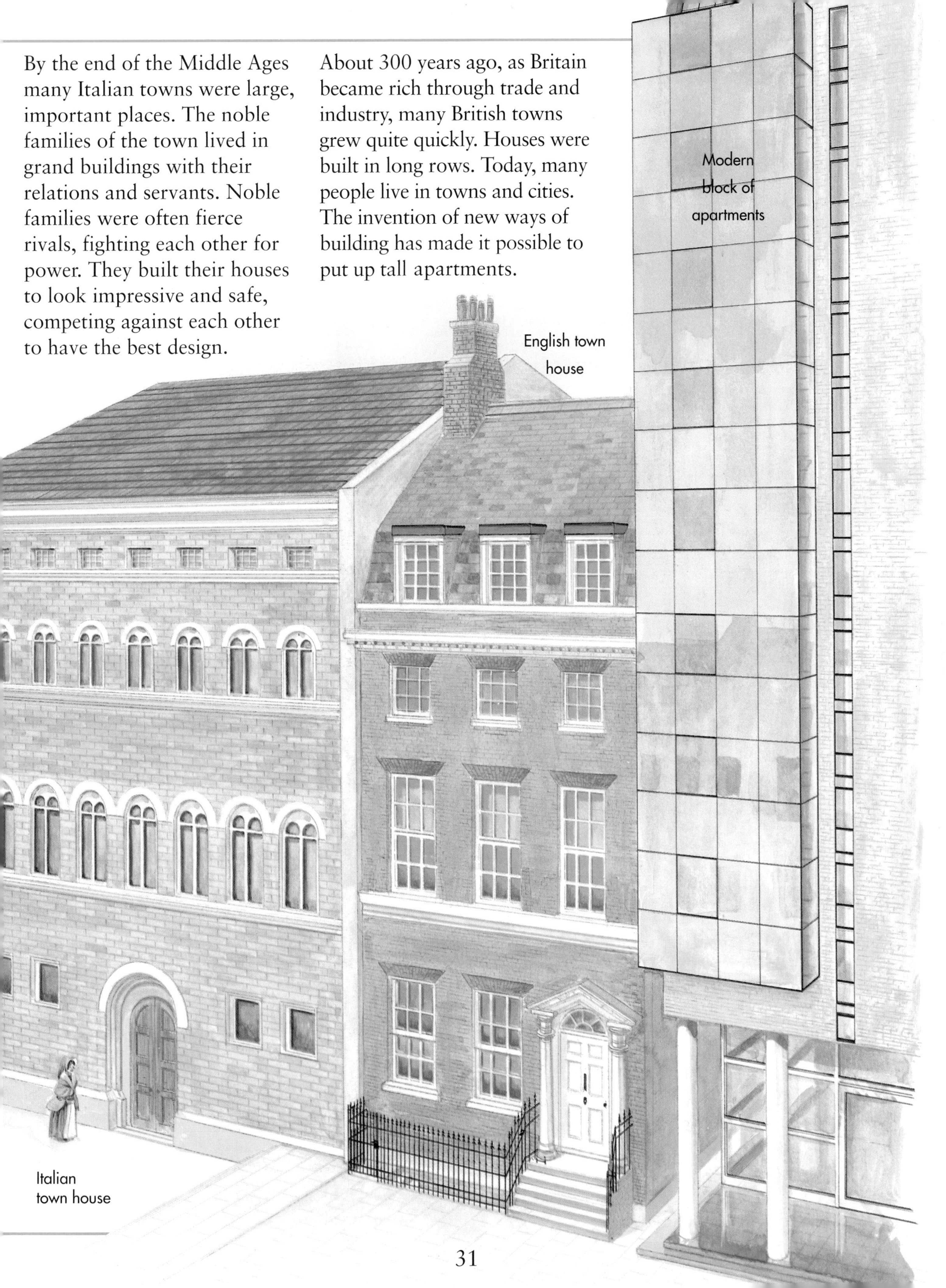

Modern block of apartments

English town house

Italian town house

31

BUILDINGS FOR THE COMMUNITY

In towns and cities people live close to one another and so can get together in large numbers for games, entertainment, learning, or to help others. All these activities need their own special buildings. Some of these buildings have to hold a lot of people at once; others are used for one purpose only, so their design is often very individual. As these buildings are usually for everyone to use, the designs can be lavish to show that people are proud of them.

Building for sport
Different sports need different shapes of building. Some sports need large playing fields, so they are played outdoors. Other sports can be played in buildings that are roofed over.

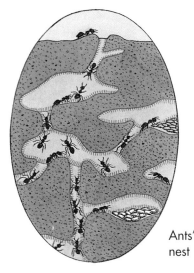
Ants' nest

Organized communities
Like humans, ants live together in organized communities. As many as 100,000 ants work together in a nest to support one another.

Buildings for entertainment
The earliest theaters were built by the ancient Greeks nearly 3000 years ago. Performances were held in the open air at religious festivals. Most modern theaters have roofs. Each building is planned for the type of performance that will take place inside. Theaters often have several halls for different types of performance.

Caring for the sick

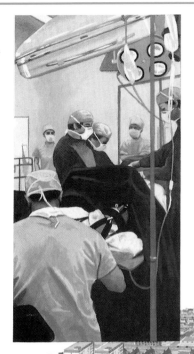

There have been buildings for the care of the sick in towns and cities for centuries. But during the present century there has been a huge improvement in medicine. Hospitals have become large buildings housing many different departments under one roof. All these departments need specially designed rooms.

Art galleries and museums

In past centuries, collections of art were always private. About 200 years ago some collectors put up special buildings to let the public see their collections. Today, art galleries and museums are an important part of public life. The design of these buildings often makes them look important. This is to show that the objects inside are also important and special.

Libraries

There have been collections of writing ever since the invention of cuneiform script. Since the invention of printing, libraries have been getting ever larger. All over the world people visit libraries to borrow and look at books for study and pleasure.

Buildings for education

Schools are usually large buildings, situated close to where people live. Schools have many classrooms, as well as halls for pupils to assemble, eat and play games.

PLACES OF WORK

For centuries, craftspeople worked at home. To do larger jobs, people would work in the open or in simple sheds. When there was constant work on large projects—such as on ships—it was worth putting up special buildings to house the work. In recent times, canals, railways and roads have made it easier to move people and the things they make. It has become usual to have special buildings for work. These buildings, or factories, are usually simple constructions that cover large spaces at a low cost.

A car factory

A modern car factory has to shelter a long assembly line. The car moves along the assembly line to have various parts added to it. The factory must protect this work without getting in the way. The building must also be designed so that there is an efficient and safe supply of electricity, air cleaning and all the other special needs for the assembly line.

Car factory

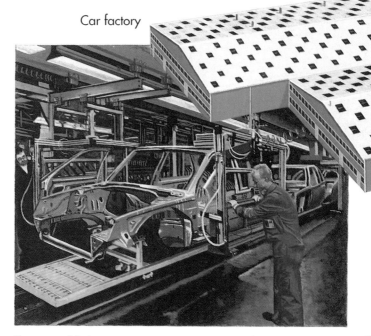

Car assembly line

Inside an aircraft hangar

Aircraft hangars are very wide sheds. Airplanes with wings up to 65 yards wide must be able to get in and out. Aircraft hangars have some of the widest roofs of any building. There cannot be any supports inside the hangar because they would get in the way of the airplanes. So special trusses and huge beams are used to cover this large area without supports.

The Arsenal in Venice

Venice in Italy was made rich by its sea trade. From the Middle Ages, all the different craftspeople involved in shipbuilding in Venice worked inside a walled area, called the Arsenal. In addition to carpenters, there were ropemakers, sailmakers, gunsmiths and many others. There were sheds for building boats and for other crafts. As many as 16,000 men worked in the Arsenal. Working together it was possible to build a warship in a day!

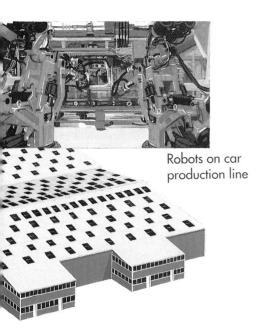

Robots on car production line

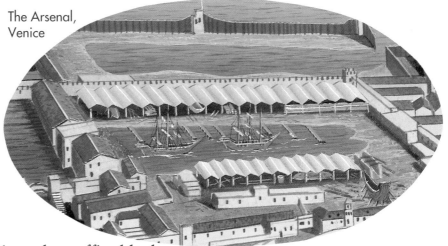

The Arsenal, Venice

A modern office block

When a modern office building is put up, there are as few walls on each floor as possible. Only the lavatories, stairs and elevators are closed in. Wires and pipes for electricity and heat are brought in through the floors and ceilings (*see page 41*). When a company moves into the building, it can put thin walls in where it wants to make offices. It can also change them around later.

Mill building

The first factories

The first modern factories were built in Britain in the 18th century. These factories were steam-powered mills for weaving cloth. The factory building was designed so that long rods could connect the machines inside the factory to the steam engine. Mill buildings were often several stories high, with one large room along the length of each story. The floors were held up by thin, cast iron columns.

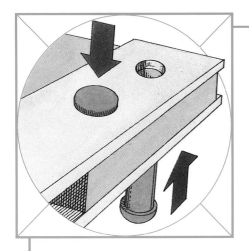

NEW MATERIALS

Until about 200 years ago, methods of building had hardly changed for centuries. There were great inventions in the past, but most buildings were still made of materials found nearby and put up in the traditional way. Around 1800, the invention of new machines and of a way of making steel, as well as the development of railways and better roads, made new types of building possible. Great changes took place very quickly, and to this day exciting new inventions are still making it possible to design and put up buildings in new ways.

The Palm House, Kew

Two hundred years ago, the manufacture of iron made it possible to put up buildings with thin beams. About 150 years ago, new developments in glass manufacture made it possible to make large sheets of glass. In 1844, the design of the Palm House in Kew Gardens brought these two inventions together.

Palm House, Kew Gardens, London

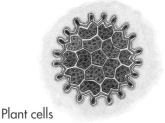

Plant cells

The geodesic dome

In the last two centuries there has been a better understanding of how different materials work when they are carrying weights. The American architect-inventor Buckminster Fuller used this knowledge to create a new structure called a geodesic dome. In 1958, the dome that he put up in Louisiana was the widest ever built. It was 128 yards across without any support inside. The frame was joined together by a method similar to the way plant cells join together for strength.

Geodesic dome, Louisiana

The Millennium Tower

About 150 years ago a way of making large beams of steel was invented. Steel is a better material for holding up buildings than cast iron because it is lighter and stronger. This makes it possible to put up very tall and wide buildings. Engineers can calculate exactly how much steel will be needed to hold up even the largest building. The world's tallest building is planned for Toyko and will be held up with a framework of steel beams. It has been designed by Sir Norman Foster and it will be 2,756 feet high.

Millennium Tower

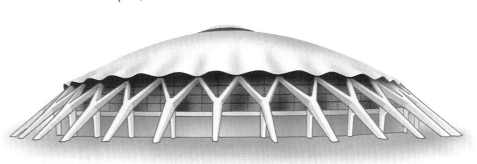

Palazzetto dello Sport, Rome

The Palazzetto dello Sport

A hundred years ago a strong building material made of a combination of concrete and steel rods was invented in France. This material is called reinforced concrete. This invention made it possible to put up long roofs which were thin and solid. The Italian engineer, Pier Luigi Nervi, designed reinforced concrete buildings. His Palazzetto dello Sport, built in Rome in 1958, is a thin concrete shell over a sports arena.

A fiberglass covering

About 50 years ago fiberglass was invented. The architect Michael Hopkins used a fiberglass cloth as a roof-covering for the Schlumberger Laboratories building. The covering is stretched like a tent between steel posts. The spider, too, uses the strength of threads to suspend its web.

Spider's web

Schlumberger Laboratories, Cambridge, England

37

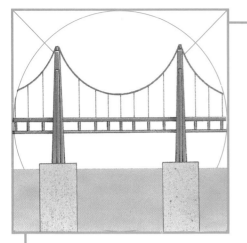

HIGHER AND LIGHTER

Early builders found ways of using cement, brick and stone to cover great spaces. But they also had to invent ways of taking the great weights of these solid roofs down to the ground. Modern materials, such as steel and fiberglass, are strong, light and flexible. This makes the problem of the weight of the roof, walls and floors much easier. The new materials make it possible to put up buildings that are higher and lighter than ever before. With these new materials, builders can imitate the strength and lightness so often found in nature.

Frame

A steel framework

Buildings made of framed wood use studs, plates, and joists to support the weight of the walls and roof. A steel frame does the same job, but steel can be made in longer lengths and more varied sizes than wood boards. Large modern buildings are put up with a frame of steel beams, and the walls and roofs are made of glass or other light materials. The steel framework of a modern building is rather like a human skeleton. The frame or bones make the building or body rigid. The frame carries all the weight of the building down to the ground on thin but strong posts, or legs.

Hong Kong and Shanghai Bank, Hong Kong

A space frame

A space frame is a special kind of steel-frame beam. Instead of crossing a space in one direction, it has a top and bottom framework separated by posts at different angles. The outside layers are held together with posts or strands crossing in several directions making it hard to bend. The whole frame works together as a complete structure.

Space frame

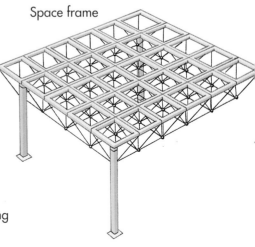

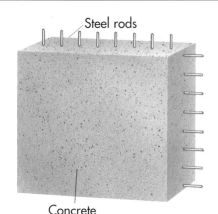
Steel rods

Concrete

Reinforced concrete

Concrete is hard to crush but breaks if bent. A steel rod is hard to stretch if pulled but bends easily if crushed. When steel is put inside concrete the two materials work together to resist both crushing and bending.

Corrugated iron

Scallop shell

Corrugated strength

A thin sheet of flat metal will bend very easily. But if the metal is shaped in a regular series of small curves it makes it more difficult to bend in one direction. Corrugated metals have been used in building as roof coverings for over 100 years. Like corrugated metal, the scallop shell is made of a brittle material that is made stronger by the little curves in its surface.

Suspension bridges

Suspension bridges are carried on steel cables hanging from towers. This type of bridge is very light, and is held up by the strength of the steel cables. The roofs of buildings can be held up in the same way (*see page 37*). People have made similar bridges for thousands of years by hanging walkways from ropes strung across rivers or ravines.

Rope bridge

Suspension bridge

Steel cables

MACHINES WE LIVE IN

Although modern houses may look as if they were built many years ago, they are full of complicated machinery to make our lives more comfortable and convenient. We light our rooms with electricity, we have central heating to keep warm, and our clothes and dishes are kept clean by machines. Workers in offices and factories also use all sorts of machines to make things, and to speak and write to one another. Office and factory buildings have elevators and escalators to move people about, air-conditioning to clean the air, and sprinkler systems to protect them from fires. Most of this machinery is hidden in roofs, cellars, floors, walls and ceilings.

Powering a house

Most houses are heated by boilers which burn gas or oil. The flame in the boiler heats water for washing and for the radiators that warm each room. The heat is turned on and off with electric thermostats and switches. The same electricity gives us light and powers other machines in the house.

Machines in the home

Machines are part of our homes. Life would be much less convenient and comfortable without stoves, fridges, freezers, washing machines, dishwashers, televisions, video recorders, and even alarm clocks.

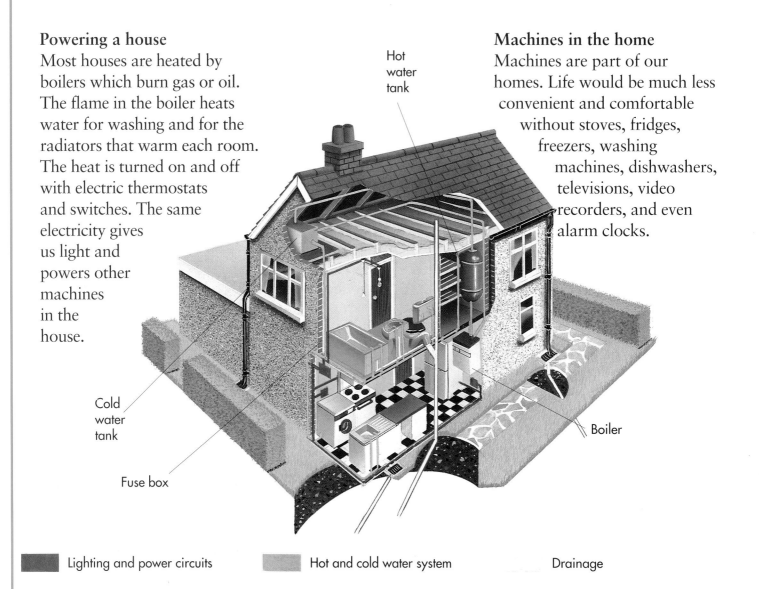

Hot water tank

Cold water tank

Fuse box

Boiler

| | Lighting and power circuits | | Hot and cold water system | Drainage |

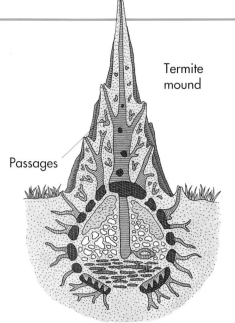

Termite mound

Passages

Keeping cool

Many modern office buildings have air-conditioning to keep the inside of the building at a comfortable temperature. On a hot day, warm air is taken away in large tubes and cool air is pumped back into the offices. Some African termites also have air-conditioning in their mounds. They keep the mounds cool by making a network of thin passages to allow air to move around constantly.

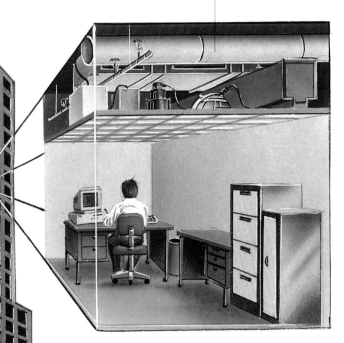

Air-conditioning ducts

Moving people about

Tall buildings must have elevators to move people about. The elevators are either pulled up and down on cables, or pushed up by hydraulic rams. There is a motor room in the roof or the basement of the building to drive the elevators.

Motor room

Cables

Elevator

Counterweight

The office machine

Office workers often live in a special world created by machines. From the equipment needed for work to the air that is breathed while working—everything is controlled by machines. A large office building is full of complicated equipment. On each desk there are computers that need an electricity supply. With so many people in one building safety is important. Large buildings have smoke detectors, fire alarms and water sprinklers.

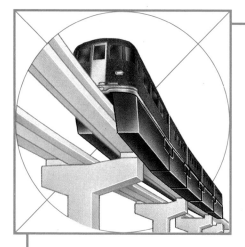

THE MODERN CITY

Over thousands of years, people have become used to the problems of living close to one another in cities. But in the 20th century, people have created new problems and found new ways of improving their lives. Changes in transport have made our cities bigger and easier to get to. Fast trains and airplanes take people from place to place in hours. In the wealthy countries of the West, most families have a car. There is a demand for more roads to drive on and more space to park. Building shopping centers and houses away from the centers of towns and cities is one way of making more room for cars, but many city centers still have traffic jams all day.

In a shopping center
New shopping centers try to make shopping pleasant and convenient. The shops are usually under cover, and the interior of the center is heated. There is a car park and elevators or escalators to upper floors. Sometimes a new shopping center is built in an old city center; sometimes a center is built out of town in a new area close to a main road.

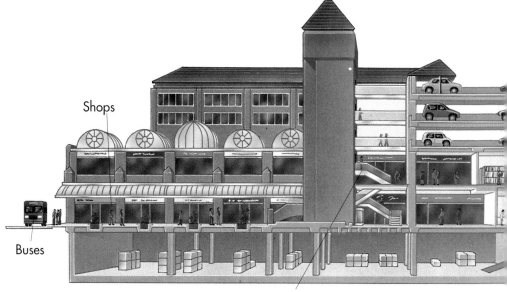

Shops

Buses

Escalators

Market

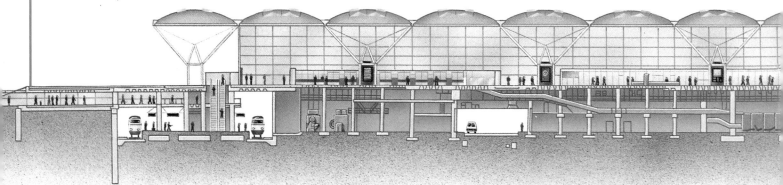

42

Old and new railway stations

Railway stations were first built nearly 200 years ago, and railways are still an important method of transport. The new Channel Tunnel station at Waterloo in London stands next to the old station. The platforms of both stations are sheltered with a glass roof held up by a steel frame. Under the glass roof are ticket offices and shops next to the platforms.

New station

Old station

Car park

Loading dock

Marina City, Chicago

Airport buildings

Airplanes are noisy, and they need long runways to take off, so airports are usually built outside cities. Airport buildings must be designed to move people on and off airplanes quickly and efficiently. There must be different areas for passengers to leave their luggage and wait for their flight. In other areas, passengers arriving off a flight need to collect their luggage and go through customs. Airlines will have offices in the building. All these areas are usually put into a single building in a series of large open halls.

Multi-purpose blocks

Some blocks of apartments are more than just a place to live. In Marina City, Chicago, it is possible to park your car and go to the hairdressers, or to the shops, launderette, swimming pool or health club without leaving the building. However, all these amenities are usually only found in large and expensive blocks of apartments.

Stansted Airport, England

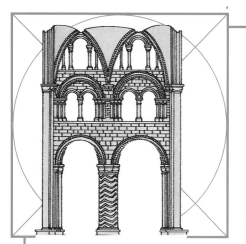

STYLES AND IDEAS

People do not just build buildings—they also make architecture. Many buildings are more than just a shelter; they are carefully designed in a particular way to fit the vision of the owner or the architect. Architecture is an art, and artists are always thinking up original ideas. In the past, designs have often been passed from generation to generation with little change. But sometimes new types of design were invented for new types of building. Sometimes, too, old designs were brought back again. This history, and the variety of different architects' styles, make architecture much more than a simple craft or science.

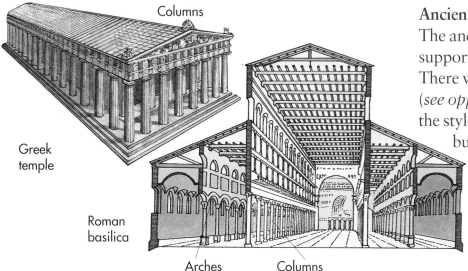

Columns

Greek temple

Roman basilica

Arches   Columns

Ancient Greece and Rome
The ancient Greeks used columns to support and decorate their buildings. There were three different types of column (*see opposite*). The type of column used set the style for the other features of the building. This was the origin of the building type we call classical. The Romans continued to use the Greek columns and they added the arch to the features used with the column.

Buildings of the Renaissance
In 1400, Italian architects started to copy buildings from ancient Rome. They added Roman columns and arches to their own buildings. This happened during a period called the Renaissance. This style spread to the whole of Europe and has been used ever since. It is called the classical style and always uses Greek and Roman features, but it has changed over the centuries.

Palazzo Strozzi, Florence

St Peter's, Rome

Villa Savoye, Poissy, France

Modernism

About 100 years ago a new style of building was invented. Some architects wanted to get rid of all ideas from the past and make something completely new. This is called Modernism. The style uses modern materials like steel, glass and concrete.

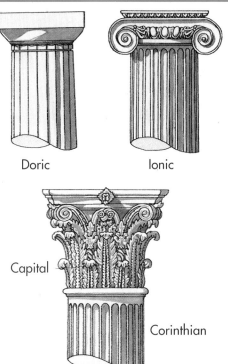
Doric   Ionic

Capital

Corinthian

The Gothic style

In the Middle Ages the largest buildings in Europe were cathedrals. Builders tried to make these buildings tall and elegant, with huge stained glass windows in the walls. The builders of cathedrals invented the most daring ways of using as little stone as possible. This style is called Gothic and can be recognized by its pointed arches.

Chartres Cathedral, France

Lloyds Building, London

Columns

Greek, Roman and Renaissance buildings use the same types of column. Buildings everywhere have them. They can be recognized by the different design at the top of the column called the capital. The types of column and the features that go with them are called Orders. There are three main Orders (*see above*).

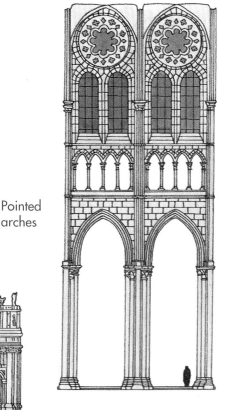
Pointed arches

Arches

In solid walls, arches are the best way of making an opening. They are also a way of recognizing a style. Roman and some Renaissance buildings often have round arches. Other types of round arch have been used on classical buildings since the Renaissance. Gothic buildings use one of the many types of pointed arch.

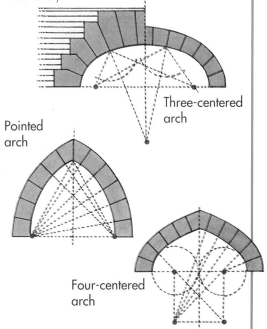
Pointed arch

Three-centered arch

Four-centered arch

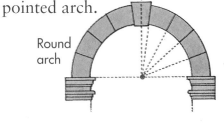
Round arch

INDEX